WORLD HISTORY

The European
Exploration of America

WORLD
HISTORY

Early River Civilizations

The Americas Before 1492

The European Exploration of America

The European Colonization of Africa

WORLD HISTORY: THE EUROPEAN EXPLORATION OF AMERICA

Library of Congress Cataloging-in-Publication Data

Nardo, Don, 1947-
The European exploration of America / by Don Nardo.
    p. cm. -- (World history)
Includes bibliographical references and index.
ISBN 978-1-59935-141-4
1. America--Discovery and exploration--European--Juvenile literature. 2.
America--History--To 1810--Juvenile literature. I. Title.
E121.N37 2010
970.01--dc22

                          2010008691

PRINTED IN THE UNITED STATES OF AMERICA
First Edition

Book cover and interior designed by:
Ed Morgan, navyblue design studio
Greensboro, NC

WORLD
HISTORY

THE EUROPEAN
EXPLORATION OF AMERICA

Dan Nardo

GREENSBORO, NORTH CAROLINA

Table of Contents

A 1602 engraving of European ships in the port of Alcapulco, Mexico

Chapter One:
The Real Discoverers of America

Each year in October, a number of American cities and towns stage parades and other celebrations in honor of Christopher Columbus. An Italian mariner sailing for Spain, he crossed the Atlantic Ocean in 1492 and landed on some islands in the Caribbean Sea. As a result of this encounter, Columbus became widely regarded as the "discoverer of America." In subsequent voyages he and other Europeans explored the coasts of North and South America, and colonization quickly followed. These are the rough outlines of the story told in countless American schoolrooms throughout the eighteenth, nineteenth, and twentieth centuries.

In recent decades, however, that traditional interpretation of history has increasingly been reexamined and challenged. In particular, various groups of Native Americans, or American Indians, have objected to it, some quite vehemently. Their argument is fairly simple and straightforward. When Columbus and his fellow Europeans arrived in the Americas, they point out, there were already millions of people living there whose ancestors had discovered America centuries before Columbus was born.

In order to emphasize this point, several Native American groups have circulated petitions with the goal of persuading the U.S. government to recognize their claims. One appeal reads in part:

> We, the undersigned, petition the President of the United States, The U.S. Congress, and The U.S. Senate to hereby change "Columbus Day" to "Native American Day." Christopher Columbus did not discover America. He discovered Native Americans living peacefully in their homeland. And, as history has taught us, Mr. Columbus was not even the first to visit America from Europe [the Vikings having visited earlier]. So then, why do we continue to disgrace Native Americans by throwing this "National Holiday" up in their faces? . . . Let us give credit where credit is due.

East-Asian Pioneers

As it turns out, Native American claims of priority in finding the Americas are well supported by evidence. Archaeologists and historians now universally recognize that up until around 15,000 years ago the only inhabitants of North and South America were animals. Then some early hunter-gatherers dwelling in Siberia, in northeastern Asia, crossed into North America. These pioneers subsequently migrated southward and over the course of thousands of years diversified into the wide range of Native American tribes that existed when the Europeans arrived.

Although many historians did not accept this explanation until fairly recently, it was by no means new. José de Acosta, a Spanish Jesuit priest and missionary, first proposed the idea. In the mid-1500s he traveled to Mexico, which his countrymen had recently conquered, and toured what are now Peru, Bolivia, and Chile. After closely studying both the geography and indigenous peoples of these regions, he wrote a book titled *Natural and Moral History of the Indians*, which detailed their social and religious customs. Acosta was keenly interested in how these peoples had gotten to the Americas in the first place, and in his book he presented what was then a bold hypothesis. E. James Dixon, director of the Maxwell Museum of Anthropology at the University of New Mexico, summarizes Acosta's viewpoint:

> After carefully and logically evaluating [the various] possibilities, Acosta concluded that the Old World and New World either were connected by land or were in close proximity in the then-unexplored high northern latitudes. Most importantly, [he] viewed the movement of humans into the Americas in conjunction with the movement of animals. After carefully considering the animal species in both the Americas and the Old World, Acosta correctly reasoned that the animals could only have passed by a land connection between the two continents.

After entering North America, Acosta suggested, the migrants slowly but steadily explored and populated the Americas until they ended up in the islands where the Spanish first encountered them. "Some peopling the lands they found," he wrote, "and other[s] seeking for new, in time they came to inhabit the Indies [Caribbean islands]."

Acosta was unable to convince many people that his theory was true. Most Europeans of his time refused to believe that the Native Americans were as ancient as he had proposed, and they formulated various scenarios to explain the presence of the Indians in the Americas. For example, one explanation held that the Indians were descended from Phoenicians, Egyptians,

Welsh, or other ancient European or Middle Eastern peoples. On sea voyages, strong winds supposedly blew some ships off course. Landing in the Americas, they settled and eventually spread across the continent. Another theory claimed that the Indians were descendants of one or more lost tribes of Israel. And still another suggested that they were the surviving humans of the fabled lost continent of Atlantis.

Another seeming strike against the Asian origins of the Indians came with a discovery made in the early 1700s. Danish navigator Vitus Bering established that Siberia and Alaska were separated by a wide expanse of freezing ocean. This body became known as the Bering Strait in his honor. The vast majority of scholars in the two centuries that followed assumed that this waterway's existence disproved the Asia-to-America migration theory that Acosta had purported.

Bering's Voyages

The existence of the Bering Strait (or Bering Sea) caused early modern scholars to doubt that the Indians originated in Asia. Danish explorer Vitus Bering (1681–1741) discovered this channel in the early eighteenth century. After serving in the Russian navy as a young man, Bering began exploring—including a voyage across the northern Asian coast in the 1720s, an expedition sponsored by the Russian government. He also sailed toward northwestern North America in 1741 and landed on an island off of the coast of Alaska. Later that year he died on another island in the sea named for him. Some two centuries passed before scientists learned that some of the land beneath that waterway had once been above sea level.

Arrival of the Paleo-Indians

It was not until the 1960s that historians gave credence to Acosta's claim that the Native Americans had migrated from Asia into North America. By this time, geological evidence had verified that sea levels had been lower at various times in the past. Specifically, about 18,000 years ago they were as much as 300 feet (91 m) lower than in modern times. Lower sea levels exposed an expanse of land that measured thousands of square miles and covered part of the present Bering Strait. It became known as the Bering Land Bridge, or Beringia.

Historians concluded that the ancient migration that Acosta had proposed occurred across this bridge; that the first people to enter North America came via Siberia. "There would have been a stretch of tundra possibly as much as 1,000 miles wide," scholar of Native American history Carl Waldman writes. At that time, "the islands of today would have been towering mountains. The big game of the Ice Age could have migrated across the land bridge. And the foremost predator among them—spear-wielding man—could have followed them. These Paleo-Siberians were the first Indians, the real discoverers of the New World."

Waldman's use of the word *tundra* is crucial. A tundra is a largely treeless region in which the subsoil is permanently frozen. At the time of the migrations in question, between 15,000 and 11,000 years ago, Beringia was a frozen wilderness. Yet enough grasses, small plants, and fresh-water ponds existed to sustain the beasts passing through and the small bands of humans following them. These beasts, including reindeer, beavers, horses, large ground sloths, and mammoths, were a major food source for the people.

Once they had made it into what are now Alaska and northern Canada, some of these hunters stayed in that region. But little by little, small splinter groups broke away and continued migrating. It is highly doubtful that they were exploring or searching for new lands. Rather, a few enterprising individuals in each succeeding generation likely intended to simply expand the tribe's hunting grounds, probably no more than into a nearby valley. Author Philip Kopper suggests,

> When they moved deliberately, it may have been to follow a herd of caribou on its annual migration. When they explored, it may have been to discover where the flocks of waterfowl nested or wintered. As for the actual pace, it might have been determined by either . . . the desire to stay put [or] the practical urge to move on. These first Americans may have lingered wherever they could make a living, which, before the rise of agriculture, meant where they found game. Even staying put, if the leader of a tribe moved his sleeping pallet only by the width of a bed each night, he would find himself ten miles away in a generation, or the distance from Canada to Nebraska in a millennium.

Clovis and Folsom Points

Both Clovis and Folsom points were designed to kill certain kinds of animals as efficiently as possible. Clovis points are roughly four to six inches long and fluted, meaning they have shallow grooves carved into the stone near the bottom. Archaeologists think that a Clovis hunter placed a rounded wooden shaft into such a groove and then tied the point to the shaft as firmly as possible. It is likely that a hunter carried some extra pointed shafts while chasing game—if one became damaged, he could replace it. Most archaeologists believe that Clovis hunters often used their weapons to bring down very large creatures, including mammoths. In contrast, Folsom points are only around two inches long and thinner than Clovis points. The size and design of the Folsom point suggests it was used primarily to kill medium-sized prey such as bison and deer.

The Clovis people skillfully crafted spear points to hunt animals such as the mammoth, bison, horse, and camel. The Ice Age hunter-gatherers lived during the Paleo-Indian period, around 13,500 years ago.

Specialists use various terms to classify these early Native Americans who spread across North America (and eventually into South America as well). One general term for them is Paleo-Indian. Other terms derive from the types of stone tools and weapons they wielded. For example, some early Indians utilized distinctive spear-tips dubbed Clovis points (after Clovis, New Mexico, where several such points were found in the 1920s). Paleo-Indians who used Clovis points are considered members of the Clovis culture. Similarly, those who used the Folsom point were part of the Folsom culture.

Finding Food

As the Clovis, Folsom, and other early Native American groups migrated southward and eastward across the continent, some of them settled down. And once they did, they tended to remain in those areas permanently, or at least for many centuries. A given group or tribe sometimes moved its village (or villages) from one sector of its region to another (often to follow the movement of game animals). But it stayed in the general area, where it adapted to the local climate, plants, and animals. The tribe also developed its own house-building methods, clothing styles, craft specialties, language, and social customs. Although trade did exist between adjacent regions, the residents of each usually viewed themselves as a separate people or nation.

Food culture distinguished the regions and tribes within them. Many early Indian groups continued the age-old hunter-gatherer lifestyle, a practice that involved killing and butchering animals of all sizes and gathering wild berries, roots, and herbs. In time, however, some tribes adopted agriculture, and some of them came to practice both hunting and farming. Hunters stalked whatever animals inhabited their local region, including small game such as rabbits and beavers, as well as all sorts of birds. When possible the hunters also stalked larger game, and in some cases a few kills would feed most of the residents of the village. After the mammoths and other giant mammals went extinct (between 12,000 and 13,000 years ago), such large game came to include elk, moose, and especially bison (or buffalo).

Tribes that hunted for a living learned not only highly effective ways of killing these beasts, but also the most efficient methods of butchering them. Joe Wheat, a preeminent archaeologist who conducted field research in Colorado for the Smithsonian Institution, closely examined the remains of some two hundred bison killed by early Indians in Colorado.

A bison grazing at Wind Cave National Park in South Dakota.

The first step in the butchering process, he said, was to roll the animal onto its belly:

> The skin was then cut down the back and pulled down on both sides of the carcass to form a kind of mat on which the meat could be placed. Directly under the skin of the back was a layer of tender meat, "the blanket of flesh"; when this was stripped away, the bison's forelegs and shoulder blades could be cut free, exposing the highly prized "hump" meat, the rib cage, and the body cavity and its prized organs. Having stripped the front legs of meat, the hunters threw the still articulated bones [away]. . . . And so it went, as the butchers cut the spine away from the pelvic girdle, then dealt with the hind legs, removing meat as they went.

Elk along a river in Yellowstone National Park in Wyoming. Early European explorers mistakenly believed that the North American elk was a moose because of its large size. The explorers were familiar with the smaller red deer of Europe.

As for those tribes that practiced farming, the exact manner and date of their discovery of agriculture is unknown.What is more certain is that some people in Mexico were growing maize, a type of corn, along with squash, beans, and pumpkins, by about 5500 BC. Knowledge of farming reached the American southwest by roughly 3500 BC, and several tribes in what is now the eastern United States were raising these crops by about 1000 BC.

The tribes that turned to farming altered their lifestyles in certain ways. They needed to be near their fields year round. So instead of periodically moving within their home region, they made their communities permanent. Frequently they erected protective wooden stockades around these villages and their family dwellings also became more permanent. The materials, shape, and construction varied from region to region. In the southeastern plains, tribes used small tree trunks and tightly packed bundles of coarse grass to build houses. "A grass house consisted of a frame of cedar poles arranged conically [coned-shaped]," a modern researcher writes, adding

> with one end anchored in the ground and the tops bound together with sapling strips. Around this frame were tied stringers of saplings, which gave the frame additional strength. (The construction of the frame was the men's responsibility.) Finally, wheat grass, coarser and denser than regular prairie grass, was lashed to this frame in bunches beginning at the bottom and continuing in overlapping rows to the peak. The attachment of the wheat grass was done by women, one working inside the house and one on the outside, using a long cottonwood needle to pass a cord back and forth between them.

Algonquian Houses

The characteristic house of another group of Native American farmers, the Algonquians, who inhabited parts of New England, was the wigwam. (Later, some white settlers came to call nearly all Indian dwellings wigwams. But technically the term applied only to Algonquian houses.) Such a structure was oval-shaped and made from saplings pushed into the ground, bent into arches, and lashed together with plant fibers. Over this frame the builders placed large bark strips. The opening that formed the doorway was covered with an animal hide or a mat constructed from woven river reeds. A typical wigwam was quite spacious—some were as large as twenty feet long and fourteen feet wide.

A hand-colored, nineteenth-century illustration of Algonquians building a wigwam

Who Owned the Land?

Whether they farmed, hunted, or did both, all Native American peoples proved to be efficient and responsible caretakers of the land. They did not over-hunt, over-fish, or destroy large tracts of forest, as many white settlers later did. This was partly because the Indians did not think that they outright owned the lands on which they lived. Rather, they believed that they were using them only with the permission of a divine force greater than themselves (frequently called the "Great Spirit" by whites).

By contrast, succeeding waves of European settlers did come to believe that they owned the lands they had "discovered." This was only one of many cultural differences between them and the indigenous people. Over time these disparities would prompt fear, hatred, violence, the eradication of several local tribes, and the permanent displacement of many others.

Chapter Two:

Norse Longships in North America

In the twentieth century scholars not only accepted the priority of the Native Americans—they also proved that other Europeans significantly predated Columbus. These earlier explorers were the Vikings, or Norse (also called Norsemen or Northmen).

They came from the cold, mountainous region of Scandinavia, lying north of continental Europe. Originally robust farmers and fishermen, they eventually took to the sea and in the late AD 700s burst into English and French waters as enterprising and frightening raiders. In the words of the late University of California scholar Erik Wahlgren:

> With appalling speed the [Viking] vessels were beached and their freight of yelling warriors discharged on shore for pillage and slaughter. . . . [Under] canny and resolute captains, the marauding foreigners operated with brutal efficiency to seize their plunder, withdrawing as they had come before resistance could be organized.

> . . . Growing decade by decade, the menace ulti-
> mately encompassed much of Europe and beyond
> and persisted, in one form or another, for almost
> three centuries.

The Vikings eventually reached, and in some cases permanently settled in, what are now Russia and Turkey in the east,
Ireland and the Shetland Islands in the west, and Spain and
northern Africa in the south.

Considering their boldness as explorers, raiders, and traders,
it is not surprising that some of the Norse continued westward beyond the Shetlands. Archaeological evidence shows
that they soon found and built towns in Iceland and Greenland.
(At the time, Greenland's southern coasts were mostly ice-free
and could support farming.) "The Vikings reached and settled
Iceland from about AD 870," one historian writes.

> In the middle of the 10th century its population
> had reached about 30,000 souls. Greenland was
> eventually sighted, but it was not until about
> 980 that an expedition landed there and that
> Erik the Red—apparently so-called because he
> was a redhead—sought settlers to colonize it.
> [He] founded the two settlements known as the
> Eastern and Western colonies, which soon had
> about 3,000 Viking inhabitants.

Journeys into the Unknown

These Viking footholds in the northern Atlantic region
were located only a few hundred miles from the northeastern coasts of North America. In about 986, only a few years
after Erik reached Greenland, a Norse merchant named Bjarni
Herjolfsson was on his way there from Norway when he was
blown off course. According to the Greenlanders' Saga, an
Icelandic document from around 1200:

> [They] sailed for three days until land was lost
> to sight below the horizon. Then the fair wind
> failed and northerly winds and fog set in, and for
> many days they had no idea what their course
> was. After that they saw the sun again [and] after
> a day's sailing they sighted land. . . . They could
> see that the country was not mountainous, but
> was well wooded and with low hills.

Sailing on, Bjarni and his men sighted two more unknown lands, one flat and forested, the other mountainous with glaciers. Finally, having decided not to make landfall in any of the three locations, they headed east and made it back to Greenland.

Hearing of the discovery of new lands lying to the southwest, other Vikings in the Greenland colonies expressed an interest in exploring them and even in colonizing them. About four years later, Leif Ericsson, son of Erik the Red, partnered with Bjarni on a new expedition. The first landmass they reached was the last one that Bjarni had visited on his earlier voyage. Leif called this rocky, icy region Helluland, meaning "Flat Stone Land." Modern scholars agree that it was most likely present-day Canada's Baffin Island. The explorers later found a flat, heavily wooded area. Leif declared, "This country shall be named after its natural resources. It shall be called Markland." This name meant "Forest Land" or "Woodland." Historians concur that the region was likely territory in today's province of Labrador.

After two more days, the voyagers came to a third expanse of land. It seemed so pleasant and inviting that they decided to build houses and spend the winter, calling their settlement Leifsbudir ("Leif's Camp"). According to the saga:

> There was no lack of salmon in the river or the
> lake, bigger salmon than they had ever seen. The
> country seemed to them so kind that no winter

fodder would be needed for livestock. There was never any frost all winter and the grass hardly withered at all. In this country, night and day were of more even length than in either Greenland or Iceland.

Soon after the landing, one of the men found grape vines, which prompted Leif to call the area Vinland. Modern archaeologists and historians have long debated the exact location of Vinland. Labrador, Newfoundland, Nova Scotia, Cape Cod (in Massachusetts), and Narragansett Bay (in Rhode Island) are only a few of the suggested sites.

An undated mid-Victorian map of Canada's Eastern provinces and the northeastern region of the United States.

Tyrkir Finds Grape Vines

In this excerpt from the Greenlanders' Saga, one of Leif's men discovers the plants that gave Vinland its name.

One evening news came that someone was missing. It was Tyrkir the Southerner.... [So they] got ready to make a search with twelve men. They had gone only a short distance from the houses when Tyrkir came walking towards them.... Leif said to him, "Why are you so late?" [Tyrkir replied] "I have some news. I found vines and grapes." [Leif asked] "Is that true?" [Tyrkir answered] "Of course it is true. Where I was born there were plenty of vines and grapes...." In the spring they made ready to leave and sailed away. Leif named the country after its natural qualities and called it Vinland.

Later Voyages to Vinland

According to two of the Viking sagas, three or four more voyages to Vinland occurred between 1000 and 1030; one was commanded by Leif's brother, Thorvald, who found the settlement at Leifsbudir. This was the first Viking expedition that encountered Native Americans. Thorvald and his men described them as "small and evil-looking," with coarse hair, "large eyes, and broad cheekbones." They called them "Skraelings," which meant "wretches" or "screechers;" the latter is likely a reference to the Indian war cries.

It is not surprising that war cries were heard, for the explorers' initial encounters with the locals were violent. The Greenlanders' Saga describes the first one this way:

On their way back to the ship they noticed three
humps on the sandy beach just in from the headland. When they went closer they found that
these were three skin [animal-hide] boats, with
three men under each of them. Thorvald and
his men divided forces and captured all of them
except one, who escaped in his boat. They killed
the other eight and returned to the headland.

In the second encounter, the Skraelings attacked in force
and the Norse warriors retreated to their ship. The Skraelings
paddled their canoes out and continued the battle, in which
Thorvald was wounded and killed. "I have a wound in my armpit," he told his men. "An arrow flew up between the gunwale
and my shield, under my arm [and it] will lead to my death."

A Norwegian ship captain named Thorfinn Karlsefni led
the next Norse expedition to Vinland. He and his crew of
sixty men and five women, along with some livestock, set out
to create a permanent colony. As Thorvald had, they found
Leifsbudir and began expanding it. Not long after landing,
one of the women, Thorfinn's wife Gudrid, gave birth to a
son, Snorri, the first known child born of European parents
in the Americas.

Also like Thorvald, Thorfinn and his men encountered
indigenous people. The first few meetings were peaceful and
involved some trading. But later one of the Vikings slew a
Skraeling—allegedly for trying to steal a weapon—and a battle ensued. The Icelandic accounts say,

The fight began and many of the Skraelings were
killed. There was one tall and handsome man
among the Skraelings and [Thorfinn] reckoned
that he must be their leader. One of the Skraelings
had picked up an axe, and after examining it for
a moment, he swung it at a man standing beside

him, who fell dead at once. The tall man then took hold of the axe [and] threw it as far as he could out into the water. Then the Skraelings fled into the forest as fast as they could.

The following spring, Thorfinn decided to leave Leifsbudir, but one or two more expeditions from Greenland returned there in the two decades that followed.

Leifsbudir Located

Archaeologists and historians have many questions about these brief Viking voyages. First, where was the settlement of Leifsbudir located? For a long time scholars assumed that the Icelandic sagas were merely collections of legends that had no basis in fact. Others felt these tales likely were based on real events and that Leif's camp would be found eventually.

This debate was finally settled in the mid-twentieth century. In 1960, Norwegian explorer Helge Ingstad and his wife, Anne, an archaeologist, found the remains of an archaic settlement at L'Anse aux Meadows, in northern Newfoundland. They compared these remains to those of Viking settlements in Greenland and Iceland in the period from 950 to 1050; the similarities were stunning.

Their excavations uncovered eight buildings and 125 artifacts. The latter included iron nails, a copper dress pin of the style worn by Viking women in that period, bone needles, whetstones for sharpening knives, pieces of rope, and a small birch-bark container. Using sophisticated modern dating methods, the Ingstads dated all of these items to approximately AD 1000 and concluded that the Liefsbudir settlement had been located at L'Anse aux Meadows. Writing in 2005, noted University of York scholar Julian D. Richards agreed:

Only a chieftain such as Leif could establish a site like this, and the scale of operations makes it

This hand-colored woodcut of a nineteeth-century illustration depicts the discovery of grapes by a Viking expedition led by Leif Ericsson in AD 1001. Ericsson named the new land Vinland.

unlikely that it is an unnamed settlement, especially given the effort that must have gone into
its construction. At the time it was built, the total
population of Greenland was only [about 2,500
to 3,000]. If the estimates are correct then L'Anse
aux Meadows was occupied by 10-20 percent of
the population of the entire Greenland colony
. . . . It seems highly unlikely that the Norse had
sufficient resources to construct a string of such
settlements.

A second important question debated by modern scholars is whether or not northern Newfoundland was Vinland.
At first glance, the wording in the sagas makes it seem as
though Leif and his men found grape vines near the settlement
of Leifsbudir. However, as archaeologist Richard Hall points
out, grapes do not grow in northern Newfoundland. He is one
of several researchers who suggest that the establishment of
Leifsbudir and the discovery of the grapes took place in two
different locales and were later unwittingly intertwined by the
author of the saga. Leifsbudir, Hall proposes, may well have
been "an explorers' and exploiters' base, a way-station from
which to range out in search of valuable natural resources that
could be brought back [to the main settlement] for storage."
In that case, Vinland may have been farther south, perhaps in
Maine or Massachusetts.

Archaeologists have also found evidence of trade between
the Vikings and various Native American peoples. An example of such trade appears in Erik the Red's Saga:

> What the natives wanted most to buy was red
> cloth; they also wanted to buy swords and spears
> . . . . In exchange for the cloth they traded gray
> pelts. The natives took a span of red cloth for
> each pelt and tied the cloth round their heads.
> The trading went on like this for a while.

Currency: Evidence of Trade

British archaeologist Richard Hall describes a Viking coin found in the remains of an ancient Indian village in Maine:

> The so-called Maine penny [is] a silver coin with a cross motif on one side and an animal design on the other. [It] was minted for the Norwegian king Olaf Kyrre (1067-93). It was found in 1957 during the excavation of a Native American site at Naskeag Point, near Brooklin in Maine, 1,250 km (775 miles) as the crow flies from L'Anse aux Meadows. The excavations established that [the settlement was] a trading place for goods collected from a widespread native trading network extending from Labrador to Pennsylvania. . . . It seems likely that the coin represents some form of contact between Scandinavians and natives, not necessarily in Maine, and that it had been brought to Naskeag Point and lost there by someone [in] the late eleventh or twelfth century.

Viking objects found in excavations of early Native American sites in Canada and Maine support the existence of such trade. A piece of medieval European chain mail (a type of armor), iron ship rivets, pieces of Viking knives, and a coin minted in medieval Norway are some of the artifacts.

North America Abandoned

A third question frequently raised by scholars is why the Vikings abandoned their ongoing exploration and settlement of northeastern North America in the early 1000s. There appear to have been a number of factors involved. First, the local Native Americans consistently attacked the newcomers, and Viking leaders likely felt that such a dangerous menace was too much to deal with on a perpetual basis. Also, the climate in Greenland and Newfoundland was growing steadily colder. This may have been due to the initial effects of the Little Ice Age, a severe cold snap that struck the northern latitudes between about 1100 and 1460. In addition, limited natural resources existed in northern Newfoundland, many of which could be imported more easily into Greenland from Scandinavia. Finally, the Norse Greenland colonies far across the Atlantic were themselves not large enough to support a major colony of their own.

Eventually, the Vikings largely abandoned Greenland, too. And the few inhabitants who decided to stay there were sorry that they did. As the great American historian Samuel E. Morison asserts:

> It is a sad picture, the gradual snuffing out of this far-away colony so gallantly planted by Erik the Red. His last descendants, hardly able to find enough food to keep alive, [waited all]

An aerial view of L'anse aux Meadows, the only known site of a Norse village in Nor
America outside of Greenland. Located on the northern tip of Newfoundland, Canad
the archaeoligical site contains the remains of eight buildings, which Norse men and
women occupied about 1,000 years ago, for between three to ten years. L'anse aux
Meadows is a UNESCO World Heritage site.

summer for the ship from Norway that meant their salvation. [But it never came.] At some time in the second half of the fifteenth century, the last Norse Greenlander died. . . . Greenland [and the Vikings' western voyages were] so forgotten by southern Europe in his day that when a Portuguese [explorer landed in Greenland] in 1500, it was mapped as a new discovery and given a new name.

Chapter Three:
Initial European Voyages to the Americas

Compared to the Native Americans and Vikings, Christopher Columbus was a latecomer to the Americas. But he and his contemporaries did not realize this fact. They viewed the Indians as ignorant, inferior savages who were merely squatting on the land and had no valid claim of either discovery or ownership. Furthermore, by the time Columbus set sail from Spain in 1492, Europe had forgotten about the Norse voyages to Vinland.

As a result, though he was not the first outsider to gaze on American territory, Columbus gained a reputation for just that. And in the process, he opened up the largest and longest age of exploration, discovery, and colonization the world had ever known. Two enormous continents—North and South America—were mapped, settled, and exploited in the three centuries that followed. The settlement of the Americas marked a crucial development in history and gave rise to the culture that is still prevalent on those continents today.

Why Columbus Sailed West

Sometime in late 1483 or early 1484, Columbus, a Genoese Italian then about thirty-three years old, approached Portugal's King John II with a bold proposal. If the king would sponsor a naval expedition, Columbus would make Portugal much richer and more powerful than it already was. He would sail west into the Atlantic Ocean and eventually reach the East Indies and Cathay (China), lands containing vast wealth and natural resources. The Portuguese were already trying to reach those lands by sailing eastward, around southern Africa. But the western route would be more direct, shorter, and easier, Columbus claimed. And once that western connection had been established, John's nation could begin trading with and exploiting these distant places.

When asked for proof of such a western connection, Columbus first cited numerous reports of strange items found in the sea. From time to time carved pieces of wood, large reeds, and pine branches had washed ashore on beaches in the Azores (off the coast of Portugal) and other islands near Europe. Similarly, the bodies of two broad-faced men, clearly not of European stock, had been found on a beach in the Azores. Columbus and others believed these objects and corpses had drifted eastward across the Atlantic from eastern Asia.

Columbus also offered "scientific" evidence in support of his claim, citing respected Italian scholar Paolo dal Pozzo Toscanelli. When asked about possible routes to the East Indies, Toscanelli had referenced a map that showed islands lying in the Atlantic between Europe and Asia:

> I have argued for [sailing west as] the shortest
> sea route from here to the Indies, where spices
> originate, which I hold to be shorter than the one
> [that involves sailing east]. . . . I have decided it
> would be easier . . . to show that route in a map
> like those that are used in navigation. [It] shows

the whole of the west, from Ireland as far south as Guinea, with all the islands that lie in between. Directly opposite them to the west is shown the beginning of the [East] Indies with the islands and places you may reach.

The Riches of Cathay

In the same letter in which he mentioned the map, Toscanelli gave this description of Cathay (China), based on reports by traders and other travelers:

This country is heavily populated, and there are many provinces and kingdoms and cities without number under the dominion of a prince called the Great Khan, which means King of Kings. He lives most of the time in the province of Cathay. His predecessors wanted very much to have relations and friendship with Christians, and two hundred years ago they sent ambassadors to the pope asking that he send many wise men and scholars to [Cathay]. . . . You can earn there not only the greatest profits but gold and silver and precious stones as well and every kind of spice in tremendous quantities, which kinds have never been brought into our part of the world.

Despite Columbus's arguments, King John turned him down. John and his advisors were well aware of the reeds and other objects that had been found on beaches. Although they agreed that these items likely came from some islands in the Atlantic, they remained unconvinced that those islands were along the path of a shorter route to the East Indies. Furthermore, they certainly had no inkling of the existence of any continents beyond Europe, Africa, and Asia. "No one among them," University of Genoa scholar Paolo E. Taviani wrote, "not Columbus nor anyone else—scholar, artist or philosopher, sailor or merchant, holy man or magician—no one in Europe imagined there could be a fourth continent."

"God, Glory, and Gold"

Having failed to persuade the Portuguese monarch to support his expedition, Columbus turned to the Spanish queen and king, Isabella I and Ferdinand II. Like King John and other European rulers who had learned of Columbus's proposition, the Spanish queen and king were hesitant to believe that a westward route to Asia was shorter and to fund Columbus's expedition. However, Columbus was drawing attention to himself, and Queen Isabella and King Ferdinand were fearful that another nation, specifically France, would eventually support Columbus. If this happened, Spain's dominance over the seas would be at risk. With this in mind, the Spanish throne decided in 1486 to support Columbus by offering him a salary and residence in their kingdom.

Over the next few years Columbus consistently pled with Ferdinand and Isabella to reconsider his proposal. After several years of negotiations, including intermittent periods when the crown cut Columbus's stipend, the queen and king finally approved of his plan. With three small ships sponsored by the Spanish crown, Columbus sailed west in early August 1492. He sighted land on October 12—the ships had reached San Salvador, one of the islands in the Bahamas.

A vintage map of the Gulf of Mexico. Columbus first landed in the Bahamas, off the coast of Florida.

Believing that he had reached the East Indies, Columbus called the original settlers of that and neighboring islands Indians. In theory, he realized, an indigenous population, if hostile, could be a serious obstacle to trade and any Spanish claims of ownership of these islands. However, he was pleased to find that the Indians posed no credible threat. To make it clear that they could easily be controlled and exploited, he wrote to the Spanish royals, saying:

> [I searched for a place] where a fort might be built. I discovered a tongue of land which . . . contained six houses. I do not, however, see the necessity of fortifying the place, as the people here are simple in war-like matters, as your Highnesses will see by those seven which I have ordered to be taken and carried to Spain in order to learn our language and return, unless your Highnesses should choose to have them all transported to Castile, or held captive in the island. I

could conquer the whole of them with fifty men,
and govern them as I pleased.

This reference to conquest foreshadowed the way in
which the Spanish and other Europeans would deal with the
Americas in the decades that followed. Columbus, Isabella,
Ferdinand, and most other Europeans of that day saw these
lands and the peoples inhabiting them merely as commodities
to be exploited. More explorers followed Columbus, and on
their heels came soldiers, colonizers, merchants, and priests.
Historians have used the saying "God, glory, and gold" to
sum up the explorers' main goals. "God" referred to the con-
version of the Native Americans to Christianity, which many
Europeans viewed as their duty. "Glory" was shorthand for
the elevated status and reputation that a conquering, colonizing nation could gain. And "gold" implied the tremendous
wealth such nations expected to amass from exploiting the
newly found territories. That wealth took many forms, including: precious metals, especially silver and gold; farmland; raw
materials, particularly timber, spices, and furs; and slaves.

Spain and Portugal, along with other countries that rapidly
followed their lead, often stopped at nothing to succeed in this
race for riches. The most visible and heinous acts they com-
mitted were those that systematically displaced, brutalized,
and/or eradicated the indigenous peoples. In 1493, for example, large numbers of Spanish settlers and soldiers arrived
on another island on which Columbus had landed—Hispan-
iola (now Haiti and the Dominican Republic). As part of their
efforts to establish towns and a valuable commercial econ-
omy, they enslaved the Indians and forced them to work on
plantations for long hours in the tropical heat. They were so
mistreated that after only twenty-two years, 80 percent of the
island's original 250,000 inhabitants were dead. Bartolome
de Las Casas, a Spaniard who witnessed these events, wrote
about the soldiers who oversaw the workers:

A replica of one of the ships sailed by Christopher Columbus

They snatched young babes from the mothers' breasts, and then dashed out the brains of those innocents against the rocks; others they cast into rivers, scoffing and jeering them. . . . [The Spanish officers also] ordered gridirons [metal barbecues] to be placed and supported with wooden forks, and putting a small fire under them, [they roasted] these miserable wretches by degrees, and with loud shrieks [the victims] at last expired [died].

The carnage continued. A little more than a century later, all of the island's original residents had been exterminated. And similar outrages occurred repeatedly across the Americas in the wake of European exploration and colonization.

Men Lacking Honor and Morality

One of Queen Isabella's courtiers, Gonzalo Fernandez de Oviedo, later described the unprincipled motives of many of the explorers, conquerors, and colonizers of the Americas:

They are the sort of men who have no intention of converting the Indians. . . . They come only to get some gold or wealth in whatever form they can obtain it. They subordinate honor, morality, and honesty to this end and apply themselves to any fraud or homicide and commit innumerable crimes.

Southern Explorations

Although Columbus had initiated a race to exploit the lands lying in the Atlantic Ocean, the full extent of those lands was still unknown. Before they could be settled and developed, they first had to be explored and mapped. In the century after Columbus's voyages, several European nations launched hundreds of exploratory expeditions. Many of these, along with the early colonizing efforts they spawned, took place in the southern reaches of the so-called New World.

Portuguese navigator Pedro Cabral led one of the first southern voyages after Columbus's. With a large contingent of thirteen ships and 1,500 men, Cabral departed Lisbon in March 1500. He aimed to establish commercial relations with parts of eastern Asia and to introduce Christianity to those areas. In April, the Portuguese fleet reached the coast of what is now Brazil, and Cabral named the first harbor he entered Porto Seguro. Not long after docking, he returned home.

Although Cabral had found a formerly unknown piece of land in the southern Atlantic, it was unclear whether it was an island or part of a larger continent. Eager to determine how large the land was, the Portuguese king hired Italian explorer and cartographer (mapmaker) Amerigo Vespucci. In 1501, Vespucci sailed down South America's eastern coast. Exactly how far he went remains uncertain; it may have been within four hundred miles of South America's southern tip. Whatever the distance was, Vespucci was convinced that the region was part of a major continent. In a letter to his former Italian employer, Lorenzo de Medici, he said:

> I have found a continent in that southern part; more populous and more full of animals than our Europe, or Asia, or Africa, and even more temperate and pleasant than any other region known to us. . . . In these most terrible dangers of the sea it pleased the Most High [God] to show

us the continent and the new countries, being another unknown world. . . . We knew that land to be a continent, and not an island, from its long beaches extending without trending round, the infinite number of inhabitants, the numerous tribes and peoples, the numerous kinds of wild animals unknown in our country, and many others never seen before by us.

Even after establishing that the continent of South America existed, no one yet knew its size and exactly what lay beyond it. Was it situated close to eastern Asia? Or did other islands and waterways lie between those two continents? These questions were partially answered by Spanish explorer Vasco Nunez de Balboa. He became famous for two important "firsts" in Europe's ongoing exploratory race. In 1510, he established Santa Maria de la Antigua del Darien, the first permanent European settlement on the mainland of the Americas. Three years later, he led an expedition across the Isthmus of Panama and became the first European to reach the Pacific Ocean by land.

Conquest of Mexico and Peru

Having determined that the Americas lay between two vast oceans, Europeans increasingly concentrated on exploring the portions of those continents that were still unmapped and mysterious. It also became common to seize control of said lands as soon as they were found. Not long after Balboa's exploits in southern Central America, the Spanish instituted this seek-and-claim policy farther north, in what came to be called Mexico.

The Spanish conquistador (soldier-adventurer) Hernan Cortes captured Mexico in 1519. Increasing numbers of conquistadors sailed to the Americas in search of gold and glory in the early 1500s. Cortes landed with a small army, equipped

The Sick Utterly Helpless

This excerpt from a surviving Aztec document describes the terrible plague—probably smallpox—that struck the capital shortly before the siege began.

A great plague broke out in Tenochtitlán. It began to spread during the thirteenth month and lasted for seventy days, striking everywhere in the city and killing a vast number of our people. Sores erupted in our faces, our breast, our bellies; we were covered with agonizing sores from head to foot. The illness was so dreadful that no one could walk or move. The sick were so utterly helpless that they could only lie on their beds like corpses.

with horses and cannons, on Mexico's eastern coast. The first Native Americans that he encountered were subjects of the Aztec Empire. Its capital, Tenochtitlan, he learned, was situated on an island in a large lake in central Mexico.

After a number of attacks, retreats, alliances, and bloody battles, Cortes marched on Tenochtitlan late in 1520. During the eighty-day siege, the Aztecs demonstrated enormous courage as they fought for their homes and way of life. But they had already been badly crippled by diseases that the Spanish had brought with them. So the city, and with it the empire, fell. The surviving Aztecs became slave-like laborers in New Spain, the vast colony that Cortes established in the region.

A modern illustration of the island city of Tenochtitlan, now Mexico City, at the time of the arrival of Hernan Cortes and his Spanish army in 1519. Founded in 1325, Tenochtitlan was surrounded by Lake Texcoco, one of the five lakes in the Valley of Mexico.

Three great earth bridges, or causeways, led into the city. Tenochtitlan was the capital city of the Aztecs and, at its peak, had an estimated population of 200,000.

Soon after Cortes established the colony of New Spain, another conquistador named Francisco Pizarro led a similar large-scale conquest of the huge Inca kingdom in Peru, in the northwestern sector of South America. In 1533 the Spanish strangled to death the Inca emperor, Atahualpa, and claimed his realm for their nation. Some Incas continued to resist colonial rule for a couple of decades, but their efforts were in vain. What seemed like onrushing tidal waves of European soldiers, settlers, merchants, and missionaries were simply too massive to counteract. And in those parts of the Americas where the Spanish and other intruders had yet to invade, the days of Native American sovereignty were numbered.

Chapter Four:
Early Journeys into
the American West

Not long after Cortes established New Spain in Mexico and Pizarro conquered the Incas in Peru, other Spaniards began to explore the areas lying farther north. Until the mid-1500s Europeans had largely ignored the vast region that would later become the United States. But once New Spain was well established, it became a base from which new expeditions could be launched northward into that region. The American west and southwest were the first areas of this land to be investigated.

At first, the main motive for exploring these areas was a lust for riches, especially gold. Every Spaniard of that era was familiar with the legend of the fabulous Seven Cities of Cibola, in which even the buildings and streets were made of gold. The exact location of these alleged cities was unknown. But Spanish traders and priests who had dealt with Indians in northern Mexico had heard compelling tales about other tribes situated farther north. Supposedly there were in these towns huge buildings filled with jewels and other valuables. Hearing these stories, a number of conquistadors and other ambitious residents of New Spain felt that these towns were the wondrous cities of Cibola.

With Colors Flying

The leader of the first major Spanish expedition to go in search of these cities was Francisco Vásquez de Coronado. A Spanish nobleman and conquistador, he had risen to the position of governor of New Spain's Nueva Galicia province. At the request of New Spain's viceroy (colonial governor), Antonio de Mendoza, Coronado assembled in early 1540 a large company of soldiers, supporting personnel, and supplies. Among them were more than three-hundred Spaniards armed with crossbows and primitive hand-held guns called arquebuses. There were also over a thousand local Indians carrying bows and spears. When everything was ready, Mendoza gave them a big send-off. According to Pedro de Castaneda, who kept a detailed record of the expedition:

> The viceroy made them a very eloquent short speech, telling them of the fidelity [loyalty] they owed to their general and showing them clearly the benefits which this expedition might afford. . . . After this was done, the army started off with its colors flying. [Mendoza] went with them for two days, and there he took leave of them, returning to New Spain with his friends. [Then] the army continued its march.

In the weeks that followed, Coronado came upon a number of villages, but all of them were small and had no gold. So the Spaniards concluded that they had not yet reached the legendary land of Cibola. In July they neared another settlement that a Spanish friar had earlier said might well be one of the seven golden cities. But once again the marchers were disappointed. They found only an impoverished cluster of mud huts that

Castaneda described as "looking as if [they] had been crumpled all up together. There are ranch houses in New Spain which make a better appearance at a distance."

The inhabitants of the village, who turned out to be Zuni Indians, suspected that the newcomers were hostile and put up a fight. During the battle Coronado was wounded and would have been killed. But at the last moment officer Don Garcia Lopez protected his leader's body with his own, saving Coronado's life. Eventually, seeing that they had no chance of defeating the intruders, the Zunis surrendered.

Capturing a Native American Village

In this passage from his account of Coronado's expedition, Pedro de Castaneda described the battle fought at the Zuni village:

These folk waited for the army, drawn up by divisions in front of the village. When they refused to have peace on the terms the interpreters extended to them, but appeared defiant, the [Spanish pushed forward] and [the Indians] were at once put to flight. The Spaniards then attacked the village, which was taken with not a little difficulty, since they held the narrow and crooked entrance. . . . But the first fury of the Spaniards could not be resisted, and in less than an hour they entered the village and captured it.

In the End, Disappointment

For several weeks Coronado was too weak from his wounds to go on. But not wanting to waste too much time, he sent out several small parties of his best men to explore various nearby regions. One group was commanded by Don Garcia Lopez, the man who had saved Coronado's life in the clash with the Zunis. Lopez and his followers headed westward for several days. They eventually came upon a river flowing at the bottom of an enormous hole in the ground—they had found the Grand Canyon and the Colorado River.

Other parties sent out by Coronado also made significant discoveries. One group of twenty-five men led by Melchior Diaz went out in search of the Pacific Ocean. Although they never reached it, they became the first Europeans to set foot in what is now California. A third party of Spaniards, this one commanded by Hernando de Alvarado, traveled eastward and found the Rio Grande, the fifth-longest river in North America. Alvarado and his men were also the first Europeans to see one of the continent's most important large mammals, the American bison.

In the end, these rivers and animals—along with a number of small villages—were all that the Coronado expedition was able to find in the regions lying north of New Spain. To his great disappointment, those journeys never led him to the fabled golden cities. In October 1541 he wrote to the Spanish king, saying:

> What I am sure of is that there is not any gold nor any other metal in all that country, and the other things of which they had told me are nothing but little villages, and in many of these they do not plant anything and do not have any houses except of skins and sticks, and they wander around with the cows [bison]; so that the account they [various Indians] gave me was false, because they wanted to persuade me to go there with

A Spanish conquistador in armor on horseback in New Spain in the 1500s, as depicted in this hand-colored woodcut of a nineteenth-century illustration

the whole force, believing that as the way was through such uninhabited deserts, and from the lack of water, they would get us where we and our horses would die of hunger.

An Astonishing Adventure

During their journey, Coronado and his men had briefly passed through what is now northern Texas. They were not the first Europeans to see the future "Lone Star" state, however. A few years before Coronado's expedition left New Spain, a single Spaniard had explored parts of southern Texas as a part of a larger and truly astonishing personal adventure. His name was Alvar Nunez Cabeza de Vaca.

In 1528, Cabeza de Vaca had served as an officer to Panfilo de Narvaez. The latter had acquired the permission of Spain's government to launch an expedition to what is now the Gulf coast of the United States. Unfortunately for Narvaez, he made some serious miscalculations that resulted in losing his ships and most of his men, as well as his own life. The last few survivors of the ill-fated group, Cabeza de Vaca among them, then drifted aimlessly on some small rafts in the Gulf of Mexico.

Eventually, the men washed ashore on an island, which they named the "Isle of Misfortune." Modern scholars think it was Galveston Island, lying off of Texas's southeastern coast. Luckily for the shipwrecked Spaniards, some local Indians came down to the beach and gave them food. Cabeza de Vaca and his companions then tried to leave on their rafts. But a huge wave struck, killing several of them. What followed took the remaining Spaniards by surprise, as told by Cabeza de Vaca himself in a long narrative he later wrote about his exploits:

> Upon seeing the disaster we had suffered, our misery and distress, the Indians sat down with us and all began to weep out of compassion for our misfortune, and for more than half an hour they wept so loud and so sincerely that it could be heard far away.

The locals were so concerned for the visitors that they took them back to their village and built a special hut for them to rest in. The Spaniards stayed the winter, during which most of them died. Meanwhile Cabeza de Vaca learned the Indians' language and closely observed their customs, which he later recorded in his narrative. (This turned out to be fortunate for posterity. That tribe, the Karankawas, later disappeared; and if not for Cabeza de Vaca, almost nothing would be known about them.)

"Great Friendship and Harmony"

Cabeza de Vaca described the indigenous people of Galveston Island, saying in part:

> The people on it are tall and well formed; they have no other weapons than bows and arrows with which they are most dexterous [skilled]. . . . Of all the people in the world, they . . . most love their children and treat them best, and should the child of one of them happen to die, parents and relatives bewail it [for a long time]. . . . Their custom is to bury the dead, except those who are medicine men among them, whom they burn. . . . Every man has a recognized wife, but the medicine men enjoy greater privileges, since they may have two or three, and among these wives there is great friendship and harmony.

This nineteenth-century illustration shows Spanish explorer Alvar Nuñez Cabeza de Vaca crossing the Great American Desert from Texas to Mexico in the early 1500s. De Vaca departed Spain for North America in 1527.

The expedition of 250 to three hundred men landed near Tampa Bay, Florida, on April 15, 1528. However, within several months of their arrival, Cabeza de Vaca was one of only four men to survive.

In time Cabeza de Vaca decided to depart the island and explore the nearby mainland. He became a merchant and for six years wandered through southern Texas trading seashells and other items with the locals. Then some Indians informed him that three other Spaniards were living in a village farther down the coast. Hurrying there, he found the three, who had also survived the Narvaez expedition. The four men now set out toward the south, trying to reach New Spain. In a new series of exploits, they gained reputations as healers, which drew sick members of several tribes to them. "Nothing was talked about in this whole country," Cabeza de Vaca wrote, "but of the wonderful cures which God, Our Lord, performed through us, and so they came from many places to be cured."

Mapping California and New Mexico

Many years after landing in Texas, Cabeza de Vaca finally made it to Mexico City and then to Spain. There he later published his memoir, titled Naufragios (Shipwreck), which for a short time made him famous. In the years that followed, other Spaniards became equally renowned for their explorations of the American West. Juan Rodriguez Cabrillo began his career working with Cortes in New Spain. In 1542, Viceroy Mendoza, the same official who had sponsored Coronado, asked Cabrillo to explore the California coast. Departing with two or three ships, the expedition reached what is now San Diego Bay in September of that year. Then Cabrillo moved northward and entered the waterway now called Monterey Bay. He might have gone on to explore and map much more, but during the voyage he suffered a leg injury, developed an infection, and died.

Another Spanish explorer who helped to bring Spanish culture and political authority to the American southwest was Juan de Onate. One of a new generation of Spaniards born in New Spain rather than in the mother country, Onate received a request from Spain's King Philip II in 1595. Philip wanted him to lead a colonizing expedition into the upper Rio Grande valley, which Coronado had passed through several decades before.

Onate managed to establish some settlements in the valley. He also claimed a huge swath of surrounding territory for Spain, calling the area New Mexico. These successes were eventually marred by scandal, however. In 1606 Onate was recalled to Spain to face charges of cruelty in discharging his duties as New Mexico's governor.

An old world map of California and Mexico

Charges of Brutality

Onate's recall to Spain in 1606 was largely based on incidents that had occurred in 1598. In that year some disagreements with the local Acoma tribe had led to a skirmish in which thirteen Spaniards had been killed. Onate retaliated in a way that even many of the local Spaniards considered overly harsh. His soldiers massacred 800 Indians, enslaved 500 Acoma women and children, and cut off the left foot of every male Acoma over the age of twenty-five. Incredibly, at least by today's standards, Onate was acquitted, although he was banned thereafter from returning to New Mexico.

From Triumph to Tragedy

One crucial asset that Mendoza, Coronado, Onate, and other Spaniards possessed during their exploits in the American southwest were horses. This gave them a significant advantage over the Indians, who did not have horses. Horses had lived in North America in prehistoric times; but these had all died out by about 8000 BC.

The first Spanish explorers and settlers in the region closely guarded their horses. There was also a law that prohibited them from selling horses to the Native Americans. In time, however, some Spaniards secretly traded the beasts to the Indians, while other Indians stole horses from poorly guarded ranches. It did not take long for the local tribes to start breeding horses and using them for traveling, hauling goods, and especially hunting. And the breeding and use of horses swiftly spread northeastward into the plains region. The Apache had horses by 1640 at the latest. And the Crow, Cheyenne, Arapaho, and Sioux had them by 1740. These latter tribes became particularly adept at killing bison from horseback. In the 1700s a new way of

An illustration of a Plains American Indian hunting on horseback

life took hold among several dozen Native American tribes. Modern scholars frequently call it the Horse and Bison Culture. "Horses produced dramatic changes," explains Paul Carlson, professor emeritus of history at Texas Tech University.

> On the southern plains, for example, the Kiowas, after the arrival of horses, shifted to a social [ladder] based on the acquisition of horses, and the idea of property took on a dramatic new meaning. New social classes appeared, [and] in a relatively short time the plains Indians passed from terrified amazement at the sight of a horse to complete equestrian mastery of the animal, and, in fact, some Indian people came to deny that there had existed a time without horses.

For the Indians of the southwest and plains, the sad irony was that the arrival of Europeans in their lands brought both triumph and tragedy. On the one hand, for example, the Spanish introduced horses, which rapidly transformed these tribes, often for the better. On the other, only a century or so later white soldiers and settlers just as quickly assaulted and dismantled the new Horse and Bison Culture. For its members, like the people of the Caribbean islands, Europe's "discovery" of America proved to be a curse rather than a blessing.

Chapter Five:

The First Europeans on the Mississippi

At about the same time that Coronado was exploring the American southwest, the first of a series of Europeans was traversing the central portion of what is now the United States. The latter region stretches from the Great Lakes in the north to the Gulf of Mexico in the south and encompasses some fourteen states today.

Essential to the exploration, settlement, and economic exploitation of this region was the mighty Mississippi River. The local Indians variously called it the "Great River" and the "Father of Waters." It was not only very long, at 2,348 miles (3,779 km), but also a major focal point of human activity and an artery for dozens of other rivers, among them the Missouri, Arkansas, Ohio, and Illinois. This combined river system made travel, communication, and trade considerably easier than was possible by land.

De Soto's Expedition

The first of these explorers known to have seen the great river was Spanish conquistador Hernando de Soto. He first arrived in the Americas in 1514. After helping in the conquest of Mexico, he served as a captain under Pizarro in Peru, where he collected enough loot to return to Spain a rich man. Then he heard about Cabeza de Vaca's journey into the mysterious lands lying north of New Spain. This inspired de Soto to return to North America, and he embarked to search for a navigable passage to China and to acquire as much gold as possible.

De Soto's expedition, consisting of about 620 Spaniards and Portuguese, nine ships, and some five hundred head of livestock, landed in western Florida in May 1539. In the two years that followed, the group made its way northward and then westward. Along the way, de Soto and his men crossed dozens of rivers and encountered numerous indigenous peoples. Some of the locals were friendly toward the outsiders; but others were more hostile, and one important battle took place in what is now Alabama. One of the Spaniards, Rodrigo Ranjel, documented it in his detailed account of the journey.

In this hand-colored illustration, Hernando de Soto's expedition is met by Chief Aquixo and his Native American warriors on the Mississippi River in 1542.

The Battle at Mablia

This is part of Ranjel's description of the skirmish fought at Mablia, which modern historians think was present-day Mobile, Alabama.

> The Indians came forth, without daring to venture far from the palisade; and in order to draw them out, [the Spaniards] pretended that those on horseback were fleeing at a gallop, withdrawing far from the ramparts, and the Indians, believing it, ventured from the town and from the palisade in their pursuit, desirous of employing their arrows, and when it was time, those on horseback turned around on their enemies, and before they could take shelter, they lanced many. . . . [Later, the Spanish] entered [the camp] through three sides, setting fire, first cutting through the palisade with axes.

Ranjel also recorded the events of early May 1541, when the band of Spaniards neared the lower reaches of the Mississippi River, in the vicinity of what is now the state of Arkansas:

> On Tuesday they went to the river that they call [the river] of Coligua, [possibly the White River] and on Wednesday likewise along the same river, and the following Thursday, which was the first of September, to Coligua, and they found the town populated, and in it they took many people and clothes and a great deal of food and much salt. It is a pleasant town among some mountains, on a gorge of a large river [the Mississippi], and from there they went at midday to kill cows [buffalo], since there are many wild ones.

Eventually, de Soto and his followers reached the Mississippi's delta, where the river empties into the Gulf. Another member of the company, Luys Hernadez de Biedma, kept a record of this part of the trip, during which the explorers again came under attack. He wrote:

> The Indians came following us downriver, until we arrived at the sea, which took nineteen days' journey. They did us much damage and wounded many people, because . . . they now had lost their fear and drew very near to shoot arrows at us. We came forth to the sea through the mouth of the river and went across a bay that the river makes, so large that we navigated three days and three nights with reasonable weather, and in all that time we did not see land.

A Priest and a Fur Trader

Having seen only the extreme lower section of the Mississippi, de Soto had no idea how far north the river and its system of tributaries extended. The first European exploration of those northern waterways did not occur for more than another century. Father Jacques Marquette, a French Jesuit missionary, instigated the venture in 1673. In the decades before, France had created a large colony—New France—in the area of Canada bordering the Great Lakes. Marquette had heard about Indian tribes living farther south, along the shores of the Mississippi and its side channels, and he wanted to establish missions in that region as part of a larger effort to spread Christianity throughout the Americas.

Teaming up with a successful French fur trader, Louis Joliet, Marquette approached French officials. The two offered to map the Mississippi region while opening it up to both religious and economic endeavors. To that end, the expedition followed Lake Michigan and then moved down the Fox River.

Crossing over to the Wisconsin River, the explorers sailed down to where it meets the Mississippi, prompting Marquette to write:

> Here we are, then, on this so renowned river, all of whose peculiar features I have endeavored to note carefully. The Mississippi River takes its rise in various lakes in the country of the northern nations. It is narrow at the place where Miskous [an old form of "Wisconsin"] empties. Its current, which flows southward, is slow and gentle. . . . We gently followed its course, which runs toward the south and southeast, as far as the 42nd degree of latitude.

Monstrous Fish

Shortly after finding the Mississippi, Marquette wrote this description of the large catfish that still inhabit that river:

> From time to time, we came upon monstrous fish, one of which struck our canoe with such violence that I thought that it was a great tree, about to break the canoe to pieces. On another occasion, we saw on the water a monster with the head of a tiger, a sharp nose like that of a wildcat, with whiskers and straight, erect ears. The head was gray and the neck quite black; but we saw no more creatures of this sort.

Jacques Marquette and Louis Joiet on the upper Mississippi River
in canoes, 1673, as depicted in a nineteenth-century illustration

Eventually, Marquette and Joliet reached Arkansas. There, fearing possible capture by Spaniards who had settled the area lying to the south, they turned back and returned to New France. Based on what the expedition had learned, the French began building forts along the northern reaches of the Mississippi, hoping that these strongholds would create a barrier between lands claimed by Spain and the English colonies located farther east.

Dreams of Empire

Another Frenchman later followed the course plotted by Marquette and Joliet. René-Robert Cavelier, Sieur de La Salle, or Robert de LaSalle, became the first European to travel most of the Mississippi's length. In 1666 La Salle arrived in Montreal, in New France. There he acquired some land and built on it a small fort and a trading post. Although his trading business was successful, he gradually felt restless and developed a desire to explore the lands lying southwest of New France. He had heard about the Mississippi River, but like everyone else, including Marquette and Joliet, he was not sure if that waterway connected with a practical passage for ships to reach the Pacific Ocean, China, and the Far East. La Salle wanted not only to find that so-called northwest passage; he also planned to help build a great French empire in the immense lands bordering the Mississippi and its tributaries.

Fortunately for La Salle, he gained an important ally who shared his vision: Louis de Buade, count of Frontenac, who had recently become governor of New France. Frontenac took the first step by getting permission from local Indians to build a fort on the northeastern shore of Lake Ontario. The fort was intended to be the portal from which French explorers and settlers would travel out into the forests and valleys beyond. With the help of his close friend, French naval officer Henri de Tonti, La Salle set to work erecting the fort, which they named Fort

Frontenac. The project was completed in 1673, the same year that Marquette and Joliet set out on their southward trek.

La Salle and Tonti began their own journey of exploration in August 1679. In a forty-five-ton boat, the *Griffin*, which Tonti had built himself, they crossed Lake Erie, then entered Lake Huron and sailed to Mackinac, situated at the junction of Lakes Huron and Michigan. Not long afterward, they made it to the Illinois River. After moving down that channel for several days, they encountered and befriended a large group of Illinois Indians. These locals allowed them to erect a small fort on a hill overlooking the river, where they spent the winter.

In the spring, La Salle decided that he lacked the manpower and supplies needed to continue the voyage. He left Tonti at the new fort and returned to New France in what turned out to be an ominous departure. While La Salle was away, Tonti's men mutinied. Then the Iroquois Indians, enemies of the Illinois, attacked. In the commotion, Tonti was badly wounded. He later wrote,

> When I was within gun-shot, the Iroquois shot at us, seized me, [and] one of them plunged a knife into my breast, wounding a rib near the heart. However, having recognized me, they carried me into the midst of the camp, and asked me what I came for. . . . All this time skirmishing was going on on both sides.

The Mississippi at Last

Fortunately for Tonti, he escaped further harm and recovered from his wounds. Also, La Salle eventually caught up with him, accompanied by a new group of twenty-two Frenchmen, eighteen Indian guides and hunters, and thirteen Indian women and children. The group moved steadily through the Ohio Valley and on February 6, 1682, made it to the intersection of the Illinois and Mississippi Rivers. Tonti described the scene:

> We went in canoes to the River Chicagou, where there is a portage which joins that of the Illinois. The rivers being frozen, we made sledges and dragged our baggage thirty leagues [78 miles] below the village of Illinois, where, finding the navigation open, we arrived at the end of January at the great River Mississippi. The distance from Chicagou was estimated at 140 leagues [364 miles].

La Salle and Tonti realized that they were not the first Europeans to see the northern Mississippi. But they decided to outdo Marquette and Joliet by following the river all the way to its mouth, a voyage that took two months. On April 6 they reached a point where the Mississippi divided into three channels; each led to the river's mouth.

At the Gulf

In his account, Tonti told about reaching the river's mouth, along the Gulf of Mexico:

> M. de la Salle sent canoes to inspect the channels; some of them went to the channel on the right hand, some to the left, and M. de la Salle chose the center. In the evening each made his report, that is to say, that the channels were very fine, wide, and deep. We encamped on the right bank, we erected the arms of the King, and returned several times to inspect the channels.

A bend in the Pearl River, near LeFleur's Bluff, site of the founding of the city of Jackson, Mississippi. The river looks much as it did when the first wanderers ventured into the area.

A Young Nation Doubled

What La Salle did next had huge consequences for the future of both his country and the future United States. He held a ceremony on the river's edge near what is now Venice, Louisiana, and claimed all the lands bordering the Mississippi as possessions of the king of France. This claim included lands, lakes, rivers, harbors, ports, towns, mines, precious metals and other resources, and the Indian peoples inhabiting the territory.

With this declaration, La Salle fulfilled his goal of opening the way for a mighty French empire in North America. French forts were built at strategic points along the Mississippi and some of its tributaries, a region that became known as Louisiana. And in the early 1700s France began colonizing and commercially exploiting that region. The French had to cede Louisiana to Spain in 1763, at the close of the Seven Years War. But shortly after 1800, France's new leader, Napoleon Bonaparte, managed to get that huge territory back.

As it happened, however, Napoleon was soon in dire need of money to support his ambitious military campaigns in Europe. In 1803 he sold Louisiana to the United States for 60 million francs—the equivalent of between 15 and 16 million American dollars. The deal, which became known as the Louisiana Purchase, almost instantly doubled the size of that young nation. The president whose administration had brokered the transaction, Thomas Jefferson, remarked:

> The property and sovereignty of the Mississippi and its waters secure an independent outlet for the produce of the western states . . . free from collision with other powers. . . . [The] fertility of the country [i.e., Louisiana], its climate and extent promise in due season [to become] important aids to our treasury [and] an ample provision for our posterity.

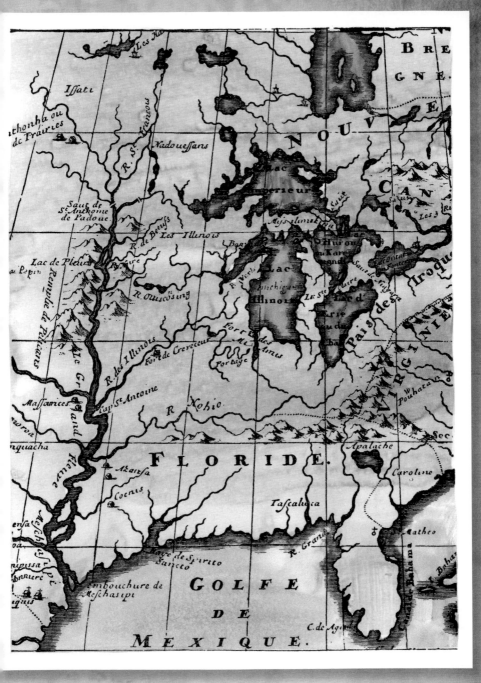

A hand-colored reproduction of part of French cleric Louis Hennepin's original
map of the Mississippi River valley and Great Lakes. The Catholic missionary is
credited with being the first white man to view Niagara Falls (in 1678).

These words proved to be an understatement, for the territory acquired in the deal eventually became the U.S. heartland. The events that transpired in that region from de Soto's time to Jefferson's remain a prime example of the tremendous impact the Age of Discovery continues to have on the modern world.

Chapter Six:
Charting the American Northeast

What is now the eastern United States, especially the northeast, stretching from New England southward to Virginia, became the first densely populated sector of colonial America. By the early 1700s, the region had hundreds of towns, as well as several large cities, including Boston, New York, and Philadelphia. Not long after the formation of the United States in 1776, the area also became the site of the new national capital, Washington, DC.

Most of the European colonies within the bounds of what became the United States had been sponsored by England. And a majority of the explorers who had paved the way for those colonies sailed for either England or France. The colonization of North America by England and France was part of a resolute effort to compete with Spain and Portugal, which by the mid-1500s had claimed huge sections of Central and South America.

At first the Spanish and Portuguese were well ahead in the race for colonies in the Americas. For instance, New Spain was a thriving colony more than eight decades before the English planted their first colony on the future eastern U.S. seaboard (at Roanoke, in Virginia). Yet over time, the pendulum of discovery, settlement, and development swung the other way. The English-speaking American northeast surpassed all competitors to become the focal point of one of the strongest, richest, and most influential countries in world history.

Early Visitors to Northeastern Waters

England's slow start in colonizing northeastern North America was not for want of trying. The first English attempt to find, map, and claim lands in that area occurred only a few years after Columbus's initial voyages to the Caribbean. In 1495, Italian navigator Giovanni Caboto, better known by the English version of his name, John Cabot, met with the English king, Henry VII. Both were anxious, as Columbus had been, to find a practical route to the East Indies and China. So they came to an agreement. And the following year Henry issued a public statement of his support for Cabot's venture. It said in part:

> We give and grant, for us and our heirs, to our well beloved John Cabot, citizen of Venice . . . full and free authority, faculty and power to sail to all parts, regions and coasts of the eastern, western and northern sea, under our banners . . . to find, discover and investigate whatsoever islands, countries, regions or provinces of heathens and infidels [non-Christians], in whatsoever part of the world placed, which before this time were unknown to all Christians. . . . John [Cabot] and his sons or their heirs and deputies may conquer, occupy, and possess whatsoever such towns, castles, cities and islands by them thus discovered.

A replica of *The Matthew*, a Tudor merchant ship sailed by the Italian-born English navigator and explorer John Cabot. *The Matthew* replica is moored in Bristol Harbor, in the United Kingdom.

Taking only one ship (compared to Columbus's three), Cabot sailed across the north Atlantic in May 1497. In June he reached Newfoundland, and some evidence suggests that shortly before making landfall he passed within a mere five miles of the ruined site of the Viking colony at L'Anse aux Meadows. Cabot knew nothing of the Viking voyages; nor did he have any inkling of where he himself had landed. The following year he tried to retrace his steps, this time with five ships, but the expedition disappeared without a trace. This was a severe financial setback for the English, who did not resume serious exploration of the Americas until many decades later. Cabot's voyages came largely to nothing at the time, and Spain and Portugal leapt further ahead in the race for overseas dominion. "Nevertheless," remarks Morison, "John Cabot's first voyage was the herald and forerunner to the English empire in North America. Like Columbus, he never learned the significance or value of his discoveries."

One service that Cabot performed for future visitors to northeastern waters was to report his sighting of schools of cod and other large fish in the area. This almost immediately attracted ambitious European fishermen, particularly from Portugal. Most of their names are unknown, but beginning at least by 1500, they piloted hundreds, if not thousands, of fishing boats across the Atlantic to ply the waters in north-eastern North America. None of these Portuguese, Spaniards, Frenchmen, Italians, and other Europeans tried to create a permanent outpost; instead, they filled their vessels to the brim with fish and headed home. Still, many made charts that became useful to later explorers and colonizers.

An Italian in New England

Meanwhile, although the English initially failed to follow up on Cabot's voyages, the French made a concerted effort to do so. In 1504, French fishing boats began to exploit the shallow coastal waters between Newfoundland and New England

Miguel in Massachusetts?

One of the little-known early Portuguese men who traveled to northeastern North America was Gaspar Cortereal, who made the trip in 1501. He never returned, and the following year his brother, Miguel, crossed the Atlantic in hopes of rescuing him. Miguel also disappeared. Centuries later, some residents of southeastern Massachusetts found unusual carvings on a large boulder called Dighton Rock. Later still, in 1929, Brown University professor Edmund B. Delabarre proposed that the carvings were Latin for "M. Cortereal 1511 by God's grace the leader of the Indians." Delabarre believed this was proof that Miguel survived his journey and became chief of a local tribe, although this theory remains controversial.

John Cabot and his English expedition landing on the shore of Labrador in 1498, as illustrated in this nineteenth-century, hand-colored woodcut.

with increasing regularity. And in 1524 the French monarchy (headed by King Francis I) invited Italian explorer Giovanni da Verrazano to investigate those waters. Verrazano entered what is now New York Harbor and saw the mouths of the rivers that empty into it, including the Hudson. Soon afterward, he sailed farther northward and charted the coasts of New England. The following passage from a letter he sent to King Francis describes part of the welcome that he and his men received on entering what is now Rhode Island's Narragansett Bay:

> We found an excellent harbor [and] before entering it we saw about [us] boats full of people who came around the ship uttering various cries of wonderment. They did not come nearer than fifty paces but stopped to look at the structure of our ship, our persons, and our clothes. Then all together they raised a loud cry which meant that they were joyful. We reassured them somewhat by imitating their gestures, and they came near enough for us to throw them a few little bells and mirrors and many trinkets, which they took and looked at, laughing, and then they confidently came on board ship.

After departing from the Rhode Island region, Verrazano continued up the coast, exploring the shores of Massachusetts and Maine. He found the residents of Massachusetts to be as impressive and friendly as those of Rhone Island. But the situation turned out to be quite different in Maine. He later recalled:

> The people were quite different from the others, for while the previous ones had been courteous in manner, these were full of crudity and vices, and were so barbarous that we could never make

A nineteenth-century illustrator's romanticized view of Giovanni da Verrazano landing in Newport Harbor in the 1500s

"Beautiful in Stature"

Verrazano later described the colorful, well-mannered indigenous leaders who came aboard his ship off the coast of Rhode Island:

> Among them were two kings, who were as beautiful of stature and build as I can possibly describe. The first was about 40 years old, the other a young man of 24, and they were dressed thus: the older man had on his naked body a stag skin, skillfully worked like damask with various embroideries; the head was bare, the hair tied back with various bands, and around the neck hung a wide chain decorated with many different-colored stones. The young man was dressed in almost the same way. These people are the most beautiful and have the most civil customs that we have found on this voyage. [Also] their manner is sweet and gentle.

any communication with them, however many signs we made to them. . . . We found no courtesy in them, and when we . . . left them, the men made all the signs of scorn and shame that any brute creature would make. Against their wishes, we penetrated two or three leagues [five to eight miles] inland with 25 armed men, and when we disembarked on the shore, they shot at us with their bows and uttered loud cries before fleeing into the woods. We did not find anything of great value in this land, except for the vast forests and some hills which could contain some metal: for we saw many natives with [copper earrings].

The Lost Colony

In the years following Verrazano's voyage into the American northeast, other Europeans continued to frequent the same waters. Among them was French explorer Jacques Cartier, who had been aboard Verrazano's ship. When Cartier launched his own expedition in 1534, it was actually his second visit to North America. Cartier mapped the Gulf of St. Lawrence and reached the future site of Montreal. He also coined the term Canada for the region lying north of New York and New England. The name derived from a local Indian word, kanata, meaning "village." Meanwhile, Portuguese, French, Italian, and English fishermen continued to ply the waters off of New England and southeastern Canada. But neither Cartier nor the fishermen created any permanent settlements.

Several decades passed before a European actually tried to establish a colony in the region. He was Sir Walter Raleigh, a favorite courtier and sea captain of Queen Elizabeth I. Elizabeth granted Raleigh a charter that authorized him to create a colony. He raised the money and organized the ships and men—more than a hundred in all. Raleigh gave his cousin Richard Grenville command over the expedition.

Gravestones commemorating the Lost Colony at Roanoke Island,
North Carolina.

The expedition reached what is now Roanoke Island, in
northern North Carolina, in August 1585. Almost immediately
the settlers ran into trouble, partly because they antagonized
the local people. One Englishman claimed that an Indian had
stolen one of his drinking cups. True or not, the settlers burned
down the Indian's village. After this incident the Indians
refused to trade with the whites. This made it difficult for the
colonists to acquire enough food, so they soon accepted an
offer from a well-known English mariner, Francis Drake, to
carry them back to England.

Despite this setback, Raleigh remained ambitious and in
1587 sent a second group of settlers, led by John White, back
to Roanoke. Once again, it proved difficult to find enough
food to sustain the colony, so White decided to go back to the
mother country and gather as many supplies as he could. For
various reasons, he ran into a number of unfortunate delays
and was unable to return to the settlement until August 1590.
Upon arriving, his worst fears were realized. All of the colonists were gone, and they had only left behind some crude
messages. Someone had carved the letters "CRO" onto a tree

trunk and another settler had carved the word "Croatoan" on the settlement's stockade. These clues led White to suspect that the colonists might have traveled to nearby Croatoan Island (now Hatteras Island). White, however, never went to the island to investigate; the sailors accompanying him were afraid that they too might disappear. The lost colonists were never heard from again.

Cape Cod and Martha's Vineyard

The second European to try colonizing the American northeast was also an Englishman: Bartholomew Gosnold, a lawyer, trader, and navigator. Although this attempt also failed, his overall efforts facilitated England's eventually successful exploitation of North America. In 1602, Gosnold sailed his vessel, the *Concord*, down the Maine and Massachusetts coasts until he found a peninsula shaped like a big fishhook. He named it Cape Cod, after seeing large schools of codfish in the nearby waters.

Gosnold conducted a cursory investigation of the Cape. Along the way he discovered large patches of wild strawberries and met with a friendly male Indian carrying a bow. Then the *Concord* sailed a few miles southward to a large island that Gosnold named Martha's Vineyard, after his daughter Martha. One of the crewmen, Gabriel Archer, who later wrote an account of the voyage, remembered:

> We saw an uninhabited island, which so afterward appeared unto us: we bore with it, and named it Martha's Vineyard; from Shoal Hope it is eight leagues [twenty-one miles] in circuit, the island is five miles, and has 41 degrees and one quarter of latitude. The place [is] most pleasant. [We] went ashore and found it full of wood, vines, gooseberry bushes, whortleberries, raspberries, eglantines, etc. . . . In this place we

saw deer: here we rode in eight fathoms near
the shore which we took great store of cod,—as
before at Cape Cod, but much better.

Moving on to the northwest of Martha's Vineyard, the vessel encountered a small but picturesque cluster of islands that
Gosnold called the Elizabeth Islands. Landing on one, the crew
built a small fort and a house. They also planted some vege-
tables and other crops and established trade relations with the
local people, who were exceedingly friendly. Gosnold hoped
to turn this modest foothold into a larger, more permanent colony. But an overall shortage of supplies forced the settlers to
abandon the site not long afterward.

Trading with the Native Americans

The Native Americans Gosnold encountered in Massachusetts
were affable and sociable and wanted to trade with the newcomers. According to Gabriel Archer's account:

Immediately there presented unto him [Gosnold]
men, women, and children, who, with all courteous
kindness entertained him, giving him certain skins
of wild beasts, which may be rich furs, tobacco, tur-
tles, hemp, artificial strings colored, chains, and
such like things as at the instant they had about
them. These are a fair-conditioned people.

A reproduction of Johannes de Laet's map of New Netherland and New England, circa 1630. De Laet was a Dutch geographer who published a *History of the New World* in 1625.

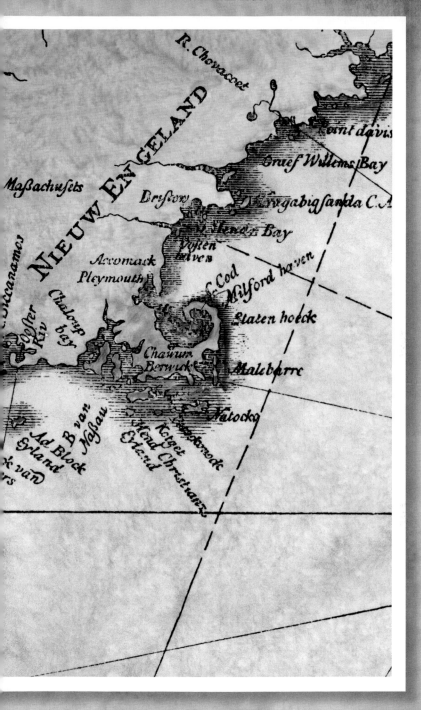

The Wheel of History

Although Gosnold was unable to establish a permanent settlement in what is now New England or the areas lying south of it, news of his voyage inspired other Europeans to do so. In 1605, for example, French explorer Samuel de Champlain mapped the region's coasts in preparation for colonization. And other nations, including the Netherlands, began planning to build their own settlements.

Once again, however, it was the English who managed to leave the biggest and most enduring imprint on the area. In 1607, English settlers established what became a permanent colony at Jamestown, in Virginia. And seven years later, English sea captain John Smith sailed along the Massachusetts coast, making accurate, useful maps as he went. In the process, he coined the term New England, which stuck in part because most of the settlers who followed him in the area were English.

Moreover, on his return to England Smith published a book detailing the landscapes, plants, animals, and Indians of the region. This volume motivated some of his fellow Englishmen to make a serious attempt to plant a permanent colony there. In 1620 this vision became a reality when a religious separatist group, the Pilgrims, founded a colony at Plymouth, just north of Cape Cod.

The creation of these and other colonies in the American northeast marked the beginning of the end of the long age of Europe's discovery of the American continents. That era propelled the emergence of the modern American nations, among them the United States, that formed in the centuries that followed.

Many people today point out that the architects of those nations often claimed credit for discoveries that were actually made millennia before by Native Americans. This fact cannot be denied, and today, historians writing about the age of discovery are careful to rectify the situation by

A photo of a replica of one of the original buildings in Jamestown,
the first English settlement in North America

acknowledging the precedence of the Native Americans in settling the Americas—to "give credit where credit is due." In this way, for the descendants of those hardy Stone Age hunters who so long ago became the first to set foot in the Americas, the great wheel of history has at last come full circle.

Timeline

BC —————————————————————————————

ca. 15,000 – ca. 11,000	Bands of hunter-gatherers from what is now Siberia migrate into North America, becoming the Native Americans.
ca. 1000	Native American tribes of the future eastern United States adopt agriculture.

AD —————————————————————————————

ca. 980	Viking leader Erik the Red lands in Greenland.
ca. 986	A Viking ship strays off course and sights North America.
ca. 1484	Italian navigator Christopher Columbus approaches the Portuguese king with a plan to reach Asia by sailing west.
1492	Sailing for Spain, Columbus reaches the West Indies.
1497	Sailing for England, John Cabot reaches North America.
1501	Italian Amerigo Vespucci sails down the eastern coast of South America.
1511	Spain establishes a colony on the island of Cuba.
1519	Spaniard Hernan Cortes leads an expedition into Mexico.
1521	Aztec capital Tenochtitlan falls to Cortes after a long siege.
1524	Italian Giovanni Verrazano sails into New York Harbor.
1528	Spaniard Francisco Pizarro lands in Peru.
1533	Pizarro orders the execution of the Inca king.
1541	Spanish explorer Francisco Coronado passes through Arizona and Texas; Spaniard Hernando de Soto is the first European to see the Mississippi River.
1572	Last Inca stronghold in Peru falls to the Spanish.
1585	English settlers reach Roanoke Island in North Carolina.
1595	Spaniard Juan de Onate colonizes territory in New Mexico.
1602	Englishman Bartholomew Gosnold lands on and names Cape Cod and Martha's Vineyard.
1607	English settlers build a permanent colony at Jamestown.
1673	Frenchmen Marquette and Joliet see the upper Mississippi River.
1682	Frenchman René-Robert Cavelier, Sieur de La Salle sails down the Mississippi River to its mouth.
ca. 1740	Several Indian tribes of the Great Plains adopt the use of horses.
1803	The United States buys Louisiana from France.

✸ Sources

CHAPTER ONE:
The Real Discoverers of America

p. 12, "We, the undersigned . . ." PetitionOnline, "Change Columbus Day to Native American Day, http://www.petitiononline.com/20021014/petition.html.

p. 13, "After carefully and logically evaluating . . ." E. James Dixon, *Quest for the Origins of the First Americans* (Albuquerque: University of New Mexico Press, 1993), 2-3.

p. 13, "Some peopling the lands . . ." Ibid., 3.

p. 15, "There would have been a stretch . . ." Carl Waldman, *Atlas of the North American Indian* (New York: Facts On File, 1985), 1.

p. 16, "When they moved deliberately . . ." Philip Kopper, *The Smithsonian Book of North American Indians* (New York: Harry N. Abrams, 1986), 31–33.

p. 19, "The skin was then cut . . ." Ibid., 44-47.

p. 22, "A grass house consisted . . ." "Grass Houses," in Frederick E. Hoxie, *Encyclopedia of North American Indians* (Boston: Houghton Mifflin, 1996), 33.

CHAPTER TWO:
Norse Longships in North America

p. 25-26, "With appalling speed . . ." Erik Wahlgren, *The Vikings and America* (London: Thames and Hudson, 1986), 29.

p. 26, "The Vikings reached and settled Iceland . . ." Rene Chartrand, Keith Durham, Mark Harrison, and Ian Heath, *The Vikings: Voyagers of Discovery and Plunder* (Oxford, England: Osprey, 2006), 67-68.

p. 27, "[They] sailed for three days . . ." Magnus Magnusson and Hermann Palsson, trans., *The Vinland Sagas* (New York: New York University Press, 1966), 52-53.

p. 27, "This country shall be named . . ." Ibid., 55.

p. 27-28, "There was no lack of salmon in the river . . ." Ibid., 56.

p. 29, "One evening news came . . ." Ibid., 57-58.

p. 29, "small and evil-looking . . ." Ibid., 98.

p. 30, "On their way back to the ship . . ." Ibid., 60.

p. 30, "I have a wound in my armpit . . ." Ibid., 61.

p. 30, "The fight began . . ." Ibid., 67.

p. 30-31, "Only a chieftain such as Leif . . ." Julian D. Richards, *The Vikings: A Very Short Introduction* (New York: Oxford University Press, 2005), 111-112.

p. 33, "an explorers' and exploiters' base . . ." Richard Hall, *The World of the Vikings* (London: Thames and Hudson, 2007), 163.

p. 33, "What the natives wanted most to buy . . ." Magnusson and Palsson, *The Vinland Sagas*, 99.

p. 34, "The so-called Maine penny . . ." Richard Hall, *The World of the Vikings*, 162.

p. 35, "It is a sad picture . . ." Samuel E. Morison, *The European Discovery of America: The Northern Voyages, A.D. 500–1600* (New York: Oxford University Press, 1993), 61.

CHAPTER THREE:
Initial European Voyages to the Americas

p. 40-41, "I have argued for [sailing west] . . ." Paolo E. Taviani, *Columbus: The Great Adventure* (New York: Orion, 1991), 53-54.

p. 41, "This country is heavily populated . . ." Ibid., 55.

p. 42, "No one among them . . ." Ibid., 58.

p. 43-44, "[I searched for a place] where a fort might be built . . ." Paul Halsall, "Christopher Columbus: Extracts from Journal," Internet Medieval Sourcebook,
http://www.fordham.edu/halsall/source/columbus1.html.

p. 46, "snatched young babes . . ." *Bartolome de Las Casas, A Brief Account of the Destruction of the Indies* (1689; Project Gutenberg, 2007),
http://www.gutenberg.org/files/20321/20321-8.txt.

p. 46, "They are the sort of men . . ." Hugh Thomas, *Rivers of Gold: The Rise of the Spanish Empire* (New York: Random House, 2005), 137.

p. 47-48, "I have found a continent . . ." Clements R. Markham, ed., trans., *The Letters of Amerigo Vespucci* (1894; Early Americas Digital Archive, 2005),
http://www.mith2.umd.edu/eada/html/display.php?docs=vespucci_letters.xml&action=show.

p. 49, "A great plague broke out . . ." "The Siege of Tenochtitlan,"
https://facultystaff.richmond.edu/~aholton/121readings_html/aztec_html/index.html.

CHAPTER FOUR:
Early Journeys into the American West

p. 54, "The viceroy made them a very eloquent short speech . . ." Pedro de Castaneda, "The Journey of Coronado" (1596; PBS Online, 2001), http://www.pbs.org/weta/thewest/resources/archives/one/corona3.htm.

p. 55, "looking as if [they] had been crumpled . . ." Ibid.

p. 55, "These folk waited for the army . . ." Ibid.

p. 56-57, "What I am sure of . . ." PBS Online, "Coronado's Report to the King of Spain," http://www.pbs.org/weta/thewest/resources/archives/one/corona9.htm.

p. 58, "Upon seeing the disaster we had suffered . . ." Fanny Bandelier, trans., "The Journey of Alvar Nunez Cabeza de Vaca," (1542; PBS Online, 2001), http://www.pbs.org/weta/thewest/resources/archives/one/cabeza.htm.

p. 59, "The people on it are tall and well formed . . ." Ibid.

p. 62, "Nothing was talked about . . ." Ibid.

p. 65, "Horses produced dramatic changes . . ." Paul H. Carlson, *The Plains Indians* (College Station: Texas A & M University Press, 1998), 37.

CHAPTER FIVE:
The First Europeans on the Mississippi

p. 69, "The Indians came forth . . ." Rodrigo Ranjel, "Account of the Northern Conquest and Discovery of Hernando de Soto," trans. John E. Worth, in The Desoto Chronicles, Vol. I, ed. Lawrence A. Clayton, Vernon J. Knight, Jr., and Edward C. Moore (1993; U.S. National Park Service

Archive, 2003), http://www.nps.gov/archive/deso/chronicles/Volume1/toc.htm.

p. 69, "On Tuesday they went to the river . . ." Ibid.

p. 70, "The Indians came following us downriver . . ." Luys Hernadez de Biedma, "Relation of the Island of Florida," trans. John E. Worth, in The Desoto Chronicles, Vol. I, http://www.nps.gov/archive/deso/chronicles/Volume1/toc.htm.

p. 71, "Here we are, then . . ." Center for Social Research, Parkland College, "Voyages of Jacques Marquette," in "Travels and Explorations of the Jesuit Missionaries in New France, 1610–1791," (2005), http://virtual.parkland.edu/lstelle1/len/Illini%20ethnohistory%20project/marquettes%20journal.htm.

p. 71, "From time to time . . ." Ibid.

p. 74, "When I was within gun-shot . . ." Henri de Tonti, "Memoir on the Discovery of the Mississippi and the Neighboring Nations," http://memory.loc.gov/cgi-bin/query/r?intldl/ascfr:@field%28DOCID+@lit%28rbfr0007_0072%29%29.

p. 75, "We went in canoes to the River Chicagou . . ." Ibid.

p. 75, "M. de la Salle sent canoes . . ." Ibid.

p. 78, "The property and sovereignty of the Mississippi . . ." Thomas Jefferson, "Third Annual Message to Congress," The Avalon Project, Yale University Law School, http://avalon.law.yale.edu/19th_century/jeffmes3.asp.

CHAPTER SIX:
Charting the American Northeast

p. 82, "We give and grant . . ." Newfoundland and Labrador Heritage Web Site Project, "Patent Granted by King Henry VII to John Cabot and His Sons, March 1496," http://www.heritage.nf.ca/exploration/1496patent.html.

p. 84, "Nevertheless, John Cabot's first voyage . . ." Morison, *The European Discovery of America, The Northern Voyages*, 192.

p. 86, "We found an excellent harbor . . ." "The Written Record of the Voyage of 1524 of Giovanni Verrazano as Recorded in a Letter to Francis I, King of France, July 8th, 1524," Barnard College, http://bc.barnard.columbia.edu/~lgordis/earlyAC/documents/verrazan.htm.

p. 86, "The people were quite different . . ." Ibid.

p. 87-88, "Among them were two kings . . ." Ibid.

p. 90, "We saw an uninhabited island . . ." Gabriel Archer, Gosnold's Settlement at Cuttyhunk, History Matters project of George Mason University (2006), http://historymatters.gmu.edu/d/6617.

p. 91, "Immediately there presented unto him . . ." Ibid.

🔀 Bibliography

Selected Books

Chartrand, Rene, Keith Durham, Mark Harrison, and Ian Heath. *The Vikings: Voyagers of Discovery and Plunder.* Oxford, England: Osprey, 2006.

Dixon, E. James. *Quest for the Origins of the First Americans.* Albuquerque: University of New Mexico Press, 1993.

Fagan, Brian M. *Ancient North America.* New York: Thames and Hudson, 2005.

Flint, Richard and Shirley C., eds. *The Coronado Expedition to Tierra Nueva.* Boulder: University Press of Colorado, 2004.

Gibson, Arrel M. *The American Indian: Prehistory to the Present.* Lexington, MA: D.C. Heath, 1980.

Hall, Richard. *The World of the Vikings.* London: Thames and Hudson, 2007.

Hassig, Ross. *Mexico and the Spanish Conquest.* Norman: University of Oklahoma Press, 2006.

Heat-Moon, *William L. Columbus in the Americas.* New York: Wiley, 2002.

Hemming, John. *The Conquest of the Incas.* New York: Harcourt Brace Jovanovich, 2003.

Horn, James, ed. *Capt. John Smith: Writings, with Other Narratives of Roanoke, Jamestown, and the First English Settlement of America.* New York: Library of America, 2007.

Leon-Portilla, Miguel, ed. *The Broken Spears: The Aztec Account of the Conquest of Mexico*. Boston: Beacon, 1992.

Magnusson, Magnus and Hermann Palsson, trans. *The Vinland Sagas*. New York: New York University Press, 1978.

Mann, Charles C. *1491: New Revelations of the Americas Before Columbus*. New York: Vintage, 2006.

McNeill, W. H. *The Rise of the West: A History of the Human Community*. Chicago: University of Chicago Press, 1992.

Morison, Samuel E. *The European Discovery of America: The Northern Voyages, A.D. 500-1600*. New York: Oxford University Press, 1993.

Parry, J. H. *The Age of Reconnaissance: Discovery, Exploration, and Settlement, 1450-1650*. Berkeley: University of California Press, 1982.

Resendez, Andre. *A Land So Strange: The Epic Journey of Cabeza de Vaca*. New York: Basic, 2009.

Richards, Julian D. *The Vikings: A Very Short Introduction*. New York: Oxford University Press, 2005.

Taylor, Alan. *American Colonies: The Settling of North America*. New York: Penguin, 2001.

Thomas, Hugh. *Rivers of Gold: The Rise of the Spanish Empire*. New York: Random House, 2005.

Wood, Michael. *Conquistadors*. Berkeley: University of California Press, 2000.

Wroth, Lawrence C., ed. *The Voyages of Giovanni da Verrazzano, 1524-1528*. New Haven: Yale University Press, 1970.

✿ Web Sites

"America's Stone Age Explorers."
http://www.pbs.org/wgbh/nova/stoneage/

"The Aztecs."
http://library.thinkquest.org/16325/y-main.html

"The Bering Land Bridge."
http://www.cabrillo.edu/~crsmith/bering.html

"Christopher Columbus and the Spanish Empire."
http://www.ucalgary.ca/applied_history/tutor/eurvoya/columbus.html

"Clovis People."
http://www.crystalinks.com/clovis.html

"Explore a Viking Village."
www.pbs.org/wgbh/nova/vikings/village.html

"Extracts from the Journal of Christopher Columbus."
http://www.fordham.edu/halsall/source/columbus1.html

"Francisco Vasquez de Coronado."
http://www.pbs.org/weta/thewest/people/a_c/coronado.htm

The Inca
http://www.mnsu.edu/emuseum/prehistory/latinamerica/south/cultures/inca.html

"John Cabot: Voyage to North America, 1497."
http://www.fordham.edu/halsall/mod/1497cabot-3docs.html

"Jose de Acosta: Pioneer of Geophysical Sciences."
http://www.faculty.fairfield.edu/jmac/sj/scientists/acosta.htm

"La Salle."
http://www.sonofthesouth.net/texas/la-salle.htm

The Spanish Empire
http://encarta.msn.com/encyclopedia_761595536/spanish_empire.html

"The Vikings."
www.viking.no/e/index.html

� Index

꩜ Picture Credits